HOW DOES IT MOVE?
FORCES AND MOTION

WITHDRAWN

HOW DO
WAVES MOVE?

AVERY ELIZABETH HURT

Cavendish
Square
New York

Published in 2019 by Cavendish Square Publishing, LLC
243 5th Avenue, Suite 136, New York, NY 10016

Library of Congress Cataloging-in-Publication Data

Names: Hurt, Avery Elizabeth, author.
Title: How do waves move? / Avery Elizabeth Hurt.
Description: First edition. | New York : Cavendish Square Publishing, [2019] |
Series: How does it move? Forces and motion | Includes bibliographical references and index. | Audience: 2-5.
Identifiers: LCCN 2017051566 (print) | LCCN 2017060329 (ebook) |
ISBN 9781502637741 (ebook) | ISBN 9781502637710 | ISBN 9781502637710 (library bound) | ISBN 9781502637727 (pbk.) | ISBN 9781502637734 (6 pack)
Subjects: LCSH: Waves–Juvenile literature.
Classification: LCC QC157 (ebook) | LCC QC157 .H87 2019 (print) | DDC 531/.1133–dc23
LC record available at https://lccn.loc.gov/2017051566

Editorial Director: David McNamara
Editor: Meghan Lamb
Copy Editor: Michele Suchomel-Casey
Associate Art Director: Amy Greenan
Designer: Alan Sliwinski
Production Coordinator: Karol Szymczuk
Photo Research: J8 Media

The photographs in this book are used by permission and through the courtesy of: Cover, p. 1 Kjell Linder/Moment/Getty Images; Throughout book Elenamiv/Shutterstock.com; p. 4 Cyndi Monaghan/Moment/Getty Images; p. 6 JohnGollop/iStock; p. 7 Pacific Ring of Fire 2004 Expedition. NOAA Office of Ocean Exploration; Dr. Bob Embley, NOAA PMEL, Chief Scientist; p. 8 Toshifumi Kitamura/AFP/Getty Images; p. 9 da-kuk/iStock; p. 10 Jong-Won Heo/Moment Open/Getty Images; p. 12 Jeff Bray/Photolibrary/Getty Images; p. 13 RonTech2000/iStock/Thinkstock; p. 14 Willard/iStock/Thinkstock; p. 15 ballycroy/E+/Getty Images; p. 16 GomezDavid/iStock; p. 17 Daniel Pangbourne/DigitalVision/Getty Images; p. 18 NOAA/Wikimedia Commons/File:Water wave diagram.jpg/CC PD; p. 19 Herbert Kratky/Getty Images; p. 20 Hulton Archive/Getty Images; p. 22 Stock Montage/Archive Photos/Getty Images; p. 23 powerofforever/iStock; p. 24 Art Collection 3/Alamy Stock Photo; p. 25 Sadatsugu Tomizawa/AFP/Getty Images; p. 26 Hero Images/Getty Images.

Printed in the United States of America

CONTENTS

Waves are powerful
and mysterious.

CHAPTER 1

WIND AND WAVES

I magine you are standing on the beach. A big wave comes toward you. Another wave is right behind it. They march toward the shore one after another.

It's fun to watch waves. And it's comforting to listen to them. But have you ever wondered what causes waves?

OCEAN IN MOTION

Most ocean waves are made by wind. Wind blows over the water. This causes **friction** between the wind and the water. Friction occurs whenever two things rub against each other. When the wind rubs against the water, the wind slows down and loses some of its **energy**.

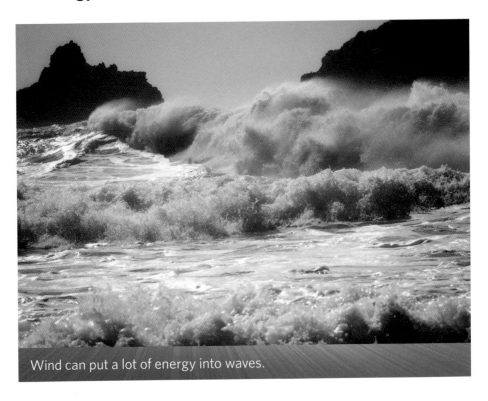

Wind can put a lot of energy into waves.

Energy is the ability to do work. Energy makes things move, like wind and waves. Where does the wind's lost energy go? It goes into the water. The new energy in the water makes waves.

Some waves are caused by movement

This undersea volcano creates big waves when it erupts.

deep under the ocean. An earthquake on the floor of the sea can cause a big wave. Waves are sometimes caused when an undersea volcano erupts. Landslides in undersea mountain ranges can cause waves, too.

A wave caused by undersea movement is called a **tsunami**. Tsunamis are giant waves. They move very fast across the open ocean. A tsunami can cross the Pacific

Tsunamis can do a lot of damage.

Ocean in less than one day. When a tsunami reaches land it can be more than 100 feet (30 meters) high.

FAST FACT

The waves at the beach are caused by winds that may have blown days before. These winds may have blown from thousands of miles away.

Remember when you pictured yourself standing on the beach? Did it seem like the water was getting closer and closer to you? If it did, that's because the tide was coming in. Tides are waves caused by the moon and the sun. Gravity is the force that pulls you toward Earth and keeps you from flying into space. The moon and the sun have gravity, too. Their gravity pulls on the water of the ocean and creates the tides.

The moon affects tides much more than the sun.

Seagulls swoop down to the waves to get their dinner.

CHAPTER 2

ENERGY ON THE MOVE

Waves might seem like big collections of water traveling across the ocean, but that's not quite right. A wave does move across the ocean. The water that makes up a wave does not. Water moves up and down. But it doesn't go forward.

DOING THE WAVE

Have you ever watched people do "the wave" at a ball game? All the people in one section of the stands raise their hands. They lower them again, all at the same time. Then the next group of people does the same. One group after another raises their hands. It looks like one big wave moving across the stadium.

These people are doing the wave—but they aren't leaving their seats.

The wave *is* moving. But the fans are standing in place as the wave passes through. The fans lift their arms. Then they lower their arms. But they do not move across the bleachers.

The fans move like the water of an ocean wave. A wave moves through the water. The

A buoy bobs gently up and down as small waves pass by.

water is part of the wave. But the water doesn't travel. Instead, it moves in an up and down motion.

You can see the same motion when watching a buoy on a lake. A passing boat makes waves in the water. The buoy bobs up and down. After the wave passes, the

Waves on a lake move up and down. They move just like waves on the ocean.

buoy stays in the same place. The buoy does not move across the lake. The water that makes up a wave moves like the buoy.

So if the water doesn't travel, what does? Energy.

PASS IT ON

There are two kinds of energy: **kinetic energy** and **potential energy**. When something is moving it has kinetic energy. Potential energy is energy that is not being used.

Imagine you're perched at the top of a slide. You have potential energy. Let go and zip down the slide. Now you have kinetic energy.

Still water has potential energy. A wave moving through water gives water kinetic energy.

Wind gives this tree kinetic energy.

Waves move through **particles**. Particles are very small bits of material. Ocean waves are made from particles of water. Wind blows on the water. That makes particles of water bump into each other. When this happens, energy moves from one water particle to the next. Waves are made by the movement of energy.

Ocean waves are just one of many types of wave.

The world is filled with different kinds of waves. There are ocean waves, light waves, and sound waves. In all of these different waves, energy moves the same way. And all waves are shaped alike.

MAKING WAVES

The bottom of the ocean is shaped like a big bowl. That's why ocean waves slosh up on shore. You can see how this works in your own bathtub. Next time you take a bath, try this. Gently slosh the bathwater back and forth. The sloshing water comes up high on the sides of the tub. With enough water in the tub, it would slosh out on the floor.

Wave experiments in the bathtub can be messy!

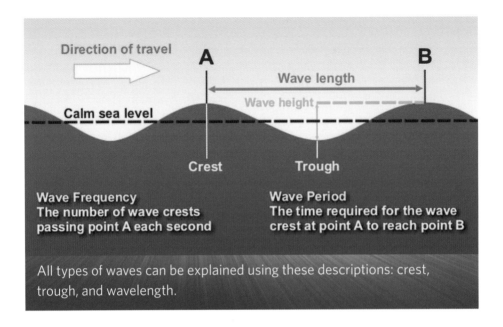

All types of waves can be explained using these descriptions: crest, trough, and wavelength.

The highest point of a wave is called the **crest**. The lowest point is called the **trough**. The distance between the peaks is called the **wavelength**. How often a wave

FAST FACT

Ocean waves have a lot of energy. People can use this energy to make electricity. One day your house lights might be powered by ocean wave energy.

repeats in a certain amount of time is its **frequency**. This is true of any wave.

Ocean waves with a high frequency and long wavelength have the most energy. Some waves are bigger than others. The faster the wind, the bigger the wave. The longer the wind blows, the bigger waves get. A light wind might make little ripples. When the wind blows hard for a long time, waves can get very big.

The same wind that makes waves makes flags ripple.

When you watch the ocean from the beach, it can be hard to see the shape of waves. It took people a long time to figure out what waves really were.

People learned how to sail boats before they learned about wind and waves.

CHAPTER 3

A DIFFICULT PROBLEM

People have always stood on the shore and watched waves. For a long time, people wondered what caused them. They saw that when the wind wasn't blowing, the water was still. When the wind picked up, waves would form. The stronger the wind was, the bigger the waves grew. People were able to see that wind caused waves. But that still didn't tell them *how* the wind caused waves.

SLOW GOING

Isaac Newton was a scientist who lived in the 1600s. He is one of the most important scientists who ever lived. Many people had wondered about waves. Newton was the first to use science and mathematics to study them.

Other scientists tried to learn how waves move. A mathematician named Leonhard Euler had some

Isaac Newton, one of the greatest scientists of all time, studied lots of things—including waves.

ideas. He came up with **equations** that showed how liquids moved. Pierre-Simon Laplace used these

Scientists such as Isaac Newton and Pierre-Simon Laplace used many instruments to do their work.

equations with ocean waves. But they did not find an answer.

More and more people began to study waves. France offered a prize to anyone who could figure out water waves. Scientists made some progress. But they still had a long way to go.

FROM PEASHOOTERS TO MOUNTAINS

George Biddell Airy was a scientist who studied waves.

George Biddell Airy was already an important scientist when he started studying waves. He was a mathematician and an **astronomer**. When he was a child, he was very shy. In school he made friends by showing other kids how to make peashooters. He was very good at math. He studied math in college and won prizes for his work. Wave movement was only one of the many subjects he studied. He also made discoveries about Earth, mountain ranges, and human vision.

TEAMWORK

In 1837, a British science group formed a **committee** to study waves. Several scientists worked together.

FAST FACT

The tallest tsunami ever recorded was 100 feet (30 meters) high. It came ashore in Alaska in 1958. It was caused by an earthquake and a landslide.

Tsunamis travel very fast and can get very big.

Scientists research and conduct experiments together. They share what they learn in published papers.

They did experiments and watched closely to see what happened. They published papers about their discoveries. This helped other scientists. This made their work go faster.

Many scientists helped with this work. But one man gets most of the credit for figuring out waves. George Biddell Airy wrote an important paper about what they'd learned. It was called "Tides and Waves." It helped everyone else understand waves better. Scientists continued to study waves. Airy's paper helped very much. Today Airy is known as the Father of Wave **Theory**.

HOW DOES IT MOVE QUIZ

1. Most waves are caused by wind. What else can cause waves?

2. What is the difference between potential energy and kinetic energy?

3. Who is known today as the Father of Wave Theory?

Answer 1: Earthquakes and volcanoes under the ocean.

Answer 2: Potential energy is not being used. Things with potential energy are still. Kinetic energy is the energy of movement. Things with kinetic energy are moving.

Answer 3: George Biddell Airy.

GLOSSARY

astronomer *A scientist who studies stars and planets.*

committee *A group of people who work to solve a problem.*

crest *The place at which a wave reaches its highest point.*

energy *The ability to move or to do work.*

equation *A statement about a relationship between things.*

frequency *The number of times a crest passes a given point.*

friction *Force from two objects rubbing against each other.*

kinetic energy *The energy of moving objects.*

particle *A basic part of matter, such as an atom.*

potential energy *Energy that is not being used.*

theory *A set of principles that explain a fact of nature.*

trough *The low point between two waves.*

tsunami *A large wave caused by undersea movement.*

wavelength *The distance between one crest and the next.*

FIND OUT MORE

BOOKS

Owen, Ruth. *Energy from Oceans and Moving Water.*
New York, NY: Rosen Publishing Group, 2013.

Squire, Anne O. *True Tsunamis.* New York, NY:
Scholastic, 2016.

WEBSITES

Easy Science for Kids: All About Currents and Waves

Easyscienceforkids.com/all-about-currents-and-waves

Information, explanations, and fun facts.

National Geographic Ocean Portal

http://kids.nationalgeographic.com/explore/ocean-portal/

A fun site filled with games, videos, and quizzes.

INDEX

ABOUT THE AUTHOR

Avery Elizabeth Hurt is the author of many books for children and young adults. Ever since she was a child growing up in Florida, she has loved to watch the sea. She enjoys learning about waves and playing in them.